NOMADS

by

Carol Bergman

Nomads

Copyright © 2014 by Carol Bergman

All Rights Reserved. No part of this publication may be transmitted or reproduced in any form by any means, graphic, electronic, or mechanical, including recording, photocopying, taping or by an information storage retrieval system now known or to be invented without the written permission of the author except in the case of brief quotations embodied in the critical articles and reviews in a magazine, newspaper, or broadcast. For more information address:

mediacs@gmail.com (212) 410-4111

A Mediacs Publication

MEDIACS

Cover design copyright © 2014 by Chloe Annetts
www.chloeartanddesign.com

Cover photograph by Carol Bergman

This is a work of fiction. All of the characters, names, incidents, organizations, and dialogue in this collection are either products of the author's imagination or are used fictitiously.

for Mildred and Gerry

dear cousins, dear friends

PREFACE

The stories in this book have been written, re-written, imagined and re-imagined, over a period of many years. For example, when I was working on "Another Day in Paradise; International Humanitarian Workers Tell Their Stories," I could only write about war or nature or myth. And everything I wrote was short.

What were these? Poems? Prose poems? Stories? Experiments? I had no idea. I had a few published and filed the rest away. And then one day, dear reader, I went to a PEN World Voices event, a reading by Lydia Davis, once married to Paul Auster and a very well-known translator with good contacts in publishing, and, lo, the three collections she had published—winning the Booker Prize for one of them—were similar to mine or, to be fair, *visa versa.*

Fiat Lux. Let there be light. I don't know where I read it but this Latin expression inspired me to curate my new collection of odd stories –because they are all stories—using Latin words and aphorisms as headings. Walking on the High Line, admiring the plantings and the view of the Mighty Hudson, a writer friend suggested that I divide the collection into sections if only as a courtesy to the reader, and though there will be some who disregard these divisions, it is still a courtesy. So I set to work knowing that every reader has the freedom to read as he or she pleases: front to back, back to front, whatever.

Fiat Lux. I love those two words, the sound of them, and the implications. Doesn't every writer suffer from the delusion that we are illuminating life in some way and that others will agree that we have done so? And we persevere in this delusion with every new work—always our best, is it not?—until we begin the next project. Suddenly we realize there is more to say and we must try to say it better. And it's odd that when we return to old work—which is what I have been doing here—there is always the sensation that either it is not good enough, or it is brilliant, that I have let in the light. Who can say? Not I.

1. ROMA

100

Teresa was waiting at the bus stop with her friend. It was a hot day and they were both wearing big straw hats and sun glasses. Teresa was elegant, dressed in black trousers and a bolero jacket with sparkles despite the hot day, and she was tall and as spindly as a crane. Lucy was tall too though stooped now, and she was still able to walk without a cane, but had trouble seeing.

The bus came and Teresa said, it's too crowded, let's wait for the next one, but Lucy wanted to get on. So they tried to get on. I wish people would realize I'm 100 years old Teresa said very loudly, but no one was listening, except for Lucy. She was younger, but not by much. These two were old friends and they were looking after each other and making friends all over the city, mostly on the buses going here and there. Oh bless her, bless her someone on line mumbled. It was moving slowly, too slowly for Teresa. She started shouting to the driver who was very busy helping a tourist get her metro card into the slot. Hey driver let us on, my friend is 100 years old, Lucy said. Did she get a card from the President, the driver asked. And Lucy said, I have it right here in my bag driver. I carry all of Teresa's documents right here in this bag. So the driver announced that Teresa had preference, he was going to get her onto his bus. She had a cane, she was a 100 years old, born in 1914, and can we imagine how long ago that was, his schedule could wait, he would explain to his supervisor that he had stopped to take a venerable New Yorker on board and that was that.

What was that, Teresa asked. I'm a bit hard of hearing, you'll give us preference, let us jump this line? I've just been to the doctor and she took some wax out of my ears. You ever had that done? It's painful let me tell you.

Suddenly everyone's hurry was suspended. The bus sighed and idled and everyone was listening to Teresa talking to the driver. Sit near me, Madam, he said. I want some of your good genes to rub off on me.

THE CONSERVATORY GARDEN

A young woman sat on a bench in the conservatory garden. It was a cloudy day, but still warm, nearly October, and the leaves were turning. She was over-dressed and she was sad. Three girls in black strapless gowns walked past. They were holding bouquets of white lilies which surely were out of season, the young woman thought. She got up and walked towards the back of the garden which was dank and chilly, hoping to find relief from the heat of the day, but a bride and groom were underneath a tree posing for pictures. The photographer ordered them to smile.

There was a pond with plantings and the young woman settled on a bench facing the pond and opened her book and began to read. A small blonde-haired boy came up to her and asked a question, but he spoke in a language she didn't understand. What he said was: *I am happy to be here.*

TOSHIBA

Although my bank is a global bank and has changed names twice in the last two years and has changed its color coordinated decor (it now has green lollipops) twice in the last two years, I still consider it my neighborhood bank which is ridiculous because I now live all the way uptown.

That said, I am still in my old 'hood many days to shop and swim, meet clients or friends, and bank. And the reason I still consider this bank my neighborhood bank is because of Toshiba. She's a teller and she always smiles as I come up to the counter and asks how I am and I ask how she is. Most importantly, her name has significance because I didn't believe her nametag at first and thought maybe it was some kind of product placement the bank had organized for TOSHIBA, the computer company, if in fact it still exists with all the mergers and such these days. But sure enough, Toshiba is Toshiba's name.

How did you get this name, I asked her one day. Meaning, what on earth were your parents thinking? They liked it, she said, and so did my grandmother who rules our family. We're from Guyana, a little village, you won't have heard of it, she said.

And then one day I called her Toyota by mistake, but because Toshiba is so good natured, she didn't mind. I realized the *faux pas* as I was leaving the counter and turned back immediately.

I can't believe I just called you Toyota I said, I really apologize. Many people do that, she said. Then the next time I went to deposit a check, she wasn't there, and I was disappointed, but the time after that she was back from her holiday in Guyana and when I asked her how it was she said that her grandmother was failing, she was very frail, and she made her promise that if she ever had a son, she would call him SONY.

SHEEP MEADOW

Though it has been raining for several days and the sky is lowering even at mid-day, we decide to meet at the Sheep Meadow Café with its black rod-iron tables where people sit for hours and read or talk and dogs lie underfoot and the steel drums play. The wind swirls and pulls the over-sized green umbrellas out of their wooden sockets and sends them roiling in a dangerous hurricane-tossed moment. Then it is quiet again, and the clouds move off quickly to the west. The lush grass on the meadow remains undisturbed, the ground soft and clear of schist and granite. Two girls toss a Frisbee and a new mother walks back and forth with her baby on her shoulder. In the distance, tall buildings glisten in the dull light and the thick-trunked trees, still heavy with foliage, sway against each other, and our hectic lives are suspended for a while inside the sweet confines of the park.

A LUCKY ESCAPE

I have just discovered that stuffing and trussing a child was once a common punishment in England and Colonial New York. In 1769, Margaret Elizabeth Garnett, ten-years-old, was stuffed and trussed in front of Trinity Church with her parents' consent. So say the documents still extant in the New York City archive in lower Manhattan. I have read them all numerous times and taken careful notes and, though it is impossible to digest all the information, and necessary to accept gaps in knowledge, I believe I have found the real story.

There are many questions remaining, however. For example: why did Margaret's parents consent? And, as we are asking: why did no one watching on that day object? Apparently there was a large crowd enjoying the spectacle. Why, then, is there no record of disapproval or dissent?

I used to believe I could learn everything from books. I read voraciously. But how do I process the accusation against Margaret Elizabeth Garnett's tongue? It was too long, it stretched across the room, and her mother wanted to snip it. Why, then, wasn't her mother—clearly sadistically insane—stuffed and trussed for entertaining these outlandish thoughts ? Why was the child punished instead?

The child recovered from her ordeal, but in her 20's she became a murderer. In fact, she murdered her parents and then escaped on a ship to Nova Scotia. Today, we might say: no wonder. But in the 18th century there was little compassion for parent killers.

A CONVERSATION WITH
A STREET VENDOR

Recently, I began a conversation with a street vendor. I needed socks. Did he have any bargains, I wanted to know. Yes, he said, three for five dollars. Then he handed me the socks.

"How did you know my size?" I asked.

"I'm intuitive that way," he said.

I had now been standing in front of his stall for at least three minutes. But I still hadn't looked at him. I was looking at the socks and feeling their weight. They were the wrong color and they were too thin, but I decided to buy them anyway. The reason was this: I looked up and saw the man's face. Though his eyes were out of alignment, he was handsome. He had high cheekbones, sensuous lips and almond skin. His hair was flecked with gray and he was tall. It was hard to figure out his age or why he moved so tentatively as he handed me the socks. His hand was trembling.

"Are you in pain?" I asked

"Isn't everyone?" he asked.

And then I had an intuition: this man was a vet, but which war? Did it even matter? And if I asked him more specifics—having assumed he was a vet—was I prepared for an answer?

Another customer had arrived. She was trying on a hat and chatting amiably. It sounded as though they knew each other, albeit only as customer and street vendor. Still, she was much friendlier than I was.

"What a winter," we all agreed.

"I've been stuck in my apartment without heat for weeks," the vendor said. "Can you tell I'm an amputee? I can't be slipping and sliding on the sidewalks."

I didn't want to know how he lost his leg. How could that be a life-affirming story? So I paid for the socks and left.

A STORY ABOUT A SUMMER MORNING IN THE CITY

Recently, I saw a man walking his dog in Central Park. It was early on a summer morning and rain fresh water was swirling off puddles in the wind, the tail of a thunderstorm. There were gulls—we get a lot of them in the city, it's an island—and ducks on the pond which we call "turtle pond." Miraculously, there are many small turtles in the pond and as I stand there watching them, I sometimes imagine a giant turtle surfacing, mother of them all. I've seen children release their captive turtles into the pond. I am sure this is illegal, but it's touching; they want them to be free.

On this morning which I am talking about, the man with his dog—a large black dog—was walking near the pond and the dog kept pulling the man closer and closer to the water. The sun was fully up and the sky had turned violet and grey. The gulls cawed and the dog barked. An elderly Indian couple—he in a turban, she with legs so bowed I thought she might collapse—walked gently by, and the man said good morning to me, rolling his r, and then he smiled. By then, the big black dog had a turtle in his mouth and there was kafuffle as we all realized we were about to witness an execution. Frantic waving and shouting at the dog's owner continued for hours, it seemed, though it was only seconds or minutes, and none of it did any good at all. The turtle was gone.

WHAT ARE WE DOING ?
WHERE HAVE WE GONE?

A lynx appeared in the garden below the Belvedere. It was Shakespeare's cat, a time traveler, camouflaged by ferns, tawny green with an elongated black bindi on its forehead. I stopped walking. Was the lynx domesticated or wild? Would it allow me to stroke its head? I said, "I will be kind to you."

I ran my finger along the meridian of its Brahmin bindi. It did not stir, but its silky fur shifted under my skin. Then it scurried away. Though the park was peopled, no one else had noticed; I was alone.

I stood for a moment. There was a breeze and then a wind. I fell forward into the newly planted petunias, vividly purple, the bard's favorite. I was bereft. The cat had disappeared, not stealthily as in life, but suddenly as in myth. One minute here, the next gone.

Later, when I told the story of the lynx in the amphitheater to the assembled throng, someone asked who I was. "I am an angel," I said. "The cat is me. It stands before you. It crouches among the flowers Shakespeare planted in his garden four hundred years ago."

WOMAN WITH BAGS

She wasn't carrying a bag, she was traveling light, she said, an old habit learned from her brothers. She was wearing an elegant large-brimmed hat and white gloves. Waiting for a bus. That's when we started talking. "I'm on my way to a fund-raiser," she said.

"I always have too many bags," I said.

I had three that day and they were weighing me down.

"A woman's plight," she said. "We are mules."

The bus arrived and we took two seats next to one another, like old friends. A middle-aged man in a suit, a goatee, and a bald head on top of a short body without any arms sat in a trance opposite us. Rubber hands poked out of his jacket, motionless. The woman turned to me and said, "I think he is praying. Let us pray for him." And she closed her eyes, put her gloved hands together on her lap, and prayed.

She got off at Lincoln Center but I was headed to the theater. I didn't want to look at the man without arms for another minute, so I fussed with my bags pretending to ready myself for departure, and then I moved to the back of the bus.

As for the rest of the evening, it was pleasant enough. The play was a good one, British actors, all well trained.

BREAST AUGMENTATION

I was traveling on the subway reading a murder mystery and sipping on a bottle of water when I looked up at the advertisements and saw a woman's breasts exposed nearly down to the nipples. My own breasts were well covered because it was cold in the train and I don't particularly like to be cold even on very hot days and also the men on the train often stare at my breasts which are very large. I am a small woman and my very large breasts make me top heavy and I have often thought of reducing them, the opposite of augmentation, of course. This advertisement was for augmentation and the woman's breasts and my breasts were very similar. We might have been sisters in the flesh, so to speak. Then I noticed that two men on my side of the subway car were also looking at the advertisement and one of them had an erection. I wondered if he was going to do anything with that erection, so to speak, and I looked away, but then I couldn't stop looking. But he didn't notice because he was looking at those augmented breasts and sighing deeply. I wondered if I should pull the emergency cord or not, but I was the only one who noticed the erection, apparently, and I was glued to my seat and couldn't even get up to move away, and the man suddenly noticed me, and then he got embarrassed, and he got up and moved away. He was a nice looking man but not my type really and too old for me and anyway I am married. Finally the subway ride was over and I got off and had a shower when I got home to cool off.

CITY NEIGHBORS

So we have a neighbor who came up the stairs to check on the noise when the apartment we are renting was being renovated. We were in the apartment looking it over with the realtor and we hadn't rented it yet, but we liked it, and knew pretty much that we wanted to rent it, but we saw that the realtor was a bit skittish when this kid—he is just a kid— came up the stairs to find out what was going on. The kid sounded kind of dopey when he spoke, a bit rough maybe, too, and he had a turned-around baseball cap on his head. A sweet face, I thought, twenty maybe.

"I just came up to see what's going on," he said.
"Just renovating," the realtor said quickly.

No way would the realtor want his clients to know there was a problem neighbor. The kid was standing at the top of the stairs, he didn't come all the way up, and though he sounded dopey, he was polite. "On something," my husband whispered. And then we got hustled into the elevator and continued our conversation about the apartment in front of the building.

Two weeks later we were in the apartment unpacking boxes when we heard a loud thumping noise, the bass on a stereo, and because it was still daylight we tried not to pay too much attention, but that's impossible, isn't it, especially if it's a disturbing sound, or music you don't like, or a sound that may be music to some, but noise to everyone else. It went on and on and I said to my husband, "We are going to have to take care of this."

Days went by and nothing. Some noise of a television, but it was hard to tell where that was coming from and then at 3 a.m. one morning, the music again, and I am up like a shot, sleep disturbed, dream interrupted. I got dressed and wrote a note. *Dear Neighbor*, all friendly , walked downstairs, and left it under the kid's door. A dog barked. That was weird; we're in a no-pet building. Two days later I saw the kid in front of the building with a dog and introduced myself properly. "Is this your dog?" I asked. "It's my uncle's. I am in my uncle's apartment," he said. "We've got leverage," I told my husband. "He's got a dog and he's probably in the apartment illegally. Sweet kid, though."

A few weeks, nothing, and then it started again, 5:30 a.m. this time. I got dressed, wrote a note, and went downstairs. The dog barked and the kid opened the door. "Really, no kidding, it's too loud?" he said. "Really," I said. "You are a sweet kid, I won't bother you again, but get a headset or something, okay?"

He agreed to try that and then he asked if I'd gotten my hands dirty putting the note under the door. He said he kept his place really clean. He said that right before I knocked on the door he'd been cleaning and brushing his teeth.

VALENCIA

I tried to explain to the tourists on the 1 train that I had never been to Valencia though I could pronounce Valen—th—ia . They were very impressed and continued to babble to me in Spanish. "Are you having a good time? Do you like New York?" Si si. There were 51 of THEM in the car—one of them held up her fingers and I counted—in the midst of rush hour on a weekday, people like me trying to get home from work—and to make matters worse, or more interesting, most of THEM were women or buff gay men in black sleeveless shirts and shaved heads talking to each other at 100 miles per hour and laughing without regard for any of the workers, such as myself, tired and trying to get home, who might have appreciated a seat. Oblivious. In their own tourist world, the subway car a party venue. Nice people, I told myself, which is why I tried to talk to them and, if I did, I thought, maybe a gallant Spaniard from Valen—th—ia would offer me a seat. "Are you having a nice time? Do you like New York?" Si, si, but no seat.

At 34th Street, Penn Station, there was more trouble. A flock of Norte Americanos dressed in white from top to toe, toting white furniture and white picnic baskets, some kind of international dining event, shoved their way onto the already crowded train. I was getting out at 28th and the door was BLOCKED so I put my fingers in my mouth and demonstrated the New York Hail a Taxi Whistle but it was lost in the din.

AS THE WORLD TURNS

Scene 1

The realtor unlocked the door and said, "An old woman just died, please forgive the condition of the apartment. It will be fully renovated."

The workers were already there, hammering and scraping. A closet door was ajar. Coats and boots, slippers, a penny, a ribbon, a frayed dog collar with an ASPCA license, no leash I could see. I was taking inventory of a stranger's life. And in the capacious step-down living room, there was a photograph of a young girl in a prom dress and another of a handsome man in a white tuxedo jacket and bow tie. If these had been the woman's children, where were they now? Why hadn't these photographs been collected?
"All of this will end up in the dumpster," I said.

My husband pressed my hand to silence me. He wanted the apartment and so did I. It was the best we had seen.

Scene 2

Piles of unused packing tape, a broken cardboard box, newsprint, bubble wrap, dust everywhere in clumps. Sweeping creates a bridge from one life to the next, each seared floorboard canonized and cleansed, an exercise in undocumented renewal. I document it here.

Scene 3

Time is a meal consumed with appetite: at dinner parties, in each other's arms, early in the morning or late at night, as the world turns.

MY DREAMS COME TRUE

It was raining this morning and the men weren't working on the retaining wall. The five-story scaffolding has been up for a while, ever since the slide last summer, but it has taken nearly a year to begin work. This is not unusual in our complex and over-burdened city, layer upon layer of infrastructure decayed or decaying since the Dutch arrived in the 17th century.

Though the noise of the hand hammering and jack hammering signals, at last, that the work has begun, it is also disturbing. Our street is a canyon and the sound ricochets. It is disconcerting to be sitting at my desk, at one end of the apartment, or go into the kitchen at the other end, and hear the sounds of the workers clearly. When the hammering stops and they are filling in cracks with a special hard bore concrete, I can even hear their conversations. "This job is my dream come true," one says. "I agree," says another.

And then they'll talk about their wives and girlfriends, and what they did to their wives and girlfriends over the weekend, or with their wives and girlfriends over the weekend. I wonder why there are no women on the job. I wonder if any of the men are gay and pretending not to be gay. I wonder if any of the workers are afraid of heights. I wonder what they'll eat for lunch.

LETTER TO THE MAYOR

Dear Mr. Mayor,

I have been meaning to write to you since you took office last January to congratulate you, of course, but also to illuminate for you various neglects perpetrated by the previous administration, neglects of which you may not be aware. I say this with all due respect as it would be impossible for any office holder in our beleaguered city to be aware of all the issues extant from previous administrations.

I know you are very busy, as are we all, Mr. Mayor, so will keep this missive short.

It's about the price of water bottles, a very egregious topic, in my view. Let me explain:

As in all other matters limning our divided city, the price of water bottles stands out, in my estimation. No underground traveler can, in their right mind, exist without a water bottle during the summer months on the subway platforms. Quite simply, it would be dangerous, for which the city might or might not have liability

Now, there are many who have purchased eco-friendly water bottles and have the foresight to fill them at home with filtered water and carry them in their bags or back packs. If we were to do a study of such water bottles, I think we would be surprised to discover the demographics of said water bottles—young. But, of course, I cannot be certain. As I am unemployed at the moment I would be happy to volunteer for this necessary survey and/or receive a small stipend (perhaps a metro card each week?).

To continue on the subject of water itself, and the bottles which contain said water. In some of the stations, there are kiosks manned by our immigrant friends from South Asia, who sell cold water bottles packed in barrels of ice. These bottles cost an outlandish $2 whereas if we had the foresight to buy a said water bottle before entering the subway, we are usually charged $1. So my question to you, Mr. Mayor, is this: Is there any way to regulate the price of water bottles under the ground? Might the city provide giveaway bottles with your Mayoral logo visible?

But there is one more egregious instance I wish to report to you here and that is of our immigrant friends from Turkey, mostly with no English at all, selling various and sundry above ground including said water bottles, usually in two sizes. (I am only talking about the smaller one here.) And these bottles Mr. Mayor can rise in price to $3, the same price as water bottles in movie houses! But because are dear immigrant friends emerge from a culture of barter and bargaining, it is possible to bargain down to $1.50, shall we say. As a native, I know this. Tourists do not. Perhaps, Mr. Mayor, this information can be provided in city publications.

I appreciate your attention on this matter. Yours sincerely, to be sure.

MESOTHERAPY

I don't know how else to explain this really: it's like psychotherapy, but different. We study the body and various body types and diagnose various ailments our clients are not aware of because they exist on the subconscious level, and then we lay them on a table in a sound-proofed room, light scented candles, and place our hands on their backs or chest—this varies depending on the diagnosis. Once the preparations of the body are complete, we chant and pray. We pray our clients will be healed, that our tender care in the sound-proofed room will be healing. We call our clients guests, men and women of all ages, but mostly women, we're not sure why. Our guests seem very satisfied with the mesotherapy and they often make an appointment for the following week as they pay and leave. I have not mentioned payment. Of course we do charge for our services, how else to pay the rent? $50 for a face only treatment, $100 for full body. Our rates are reasonable and competitive, I am sure you will agree. Thank you for your inquiry.

CITY ENSEMBLE

Always there is something I want to say about kinship, but when I went roaming through the city alone that hot summer, I wondered where my friends were, even though I'd emailed all of them and texted a few and had a response or two. Why we are so afflicted with self-pity? Or why am I? My dears, it is tasteless.

So let me begin again: At daybreak, the pavements of the city are dark until the workers scurry to the train stations and bus stops and the Con-Ed guys—and occasionally a girl these days—set up their orange warning cones and lift the manhole covers and search for skewered wires and broken piping underneath the skin of the streets, heavy with infrastructure and history. And, one day, there are spectators—an audience—leaning into a police barrier around one of these holes and there is an abundance of concern as a man surfaces from the hole with wires around his neck gasping for air, and we all move forward to assist him. We are as eloquent in this action as we were on the day The Towers fell . No one was okay that day, but today this man will be okay, the ambulance has arrived. It is only when this small crisis is over that I hear the trombone and see the musicians on the steps of the church blowing their horns, beating their drums, pausing, playing again. We—the city dwellers—could not ask for a more inventive consolation than their melodic song.

CITY NIGHT

A friend called to remind me to leave the apartment and look up at the unobstructed sky. The moon was full that night, though it was cloudy and hard to see in its fullness, even from the Sheep Meadow in Central Park. Then it appeared, bulbous and glowing, surrounded by constellations, the sun's courtiers.

The stillness of the meadow was almost unbearable, everyone looking up at the moon. I could not stay any longer so glorious was this vision.

I left the park and meandered back towards my dank apartment. I heard crickets humming, chirping and conversing in their cricket language. A couple, standing by an open window, were arguing about a disappointing vacation. Fortunately, the crickets were louder and more insistent and the moon, illuminated by the invisible sun, obliterated all shadows on the nearly deserted street.

CITY HAWKS

Take me along the river to see the nesting hawks, they who sit on the nest taking turns. May their patience remind us to stand silently and be kind to one another.

Notice the three chicks, you who rush to and from work each day and never stop.

Notice these hawks in the midst of our city lives; glorious birds watching over us.

2. INTER ALIA

HER SUITCASE WAS BLOOMING

A young woman was carrying a small gray suitcase with pink flowers etched into it. She was wearing a brown cloche hat, a brown jacket without buttons (I could see the torn threads), a brown skirt, brown stockings and sturdy brown shoes with a small square heel. I admired her simplicity and certainty as she walked across the square past the café where I was having tea and cookies. I called out to her: Please join me. But she did not hear me, or perhaps she chose to ignore me, or perhaps she did not speak my language. She walked on, not a jaunty stride exactly, but purposeful. The sun caught the etched blossoms on her suitcase and brought them to life inside me.

THE STREAM'S LESSON

Today I saw a woman standing in the streambed, water to her shins. It is January and there are ice floes. I decided it was a dangerous situation so I took off my sturdy walking shoes and wool socks and waded in. I called to her, oh Madam, oh Madam, because she was an older woman, older than I am certainly. But she did not hear me, or preferred not to hear me.

I stood beside her—to her left, to be exact—and looked down into the rushing water. The tips of my toes, once manicured and tended, were now embedded in polished pebbles. I was unable to move, paralyzed. Finally, I raised one foot, then another, and I said to the woman: The weather is changing, the clouds are shifting. Suddenly there were razor sparks of light, and then a rainbow. It's a sign, I said.

If this woman was an imbecile, I was no more intelligent. Clearly, she did not want to be rescued.

IS SHE BLIND?

Ava and Elena are watching the Spanish soaps when I arrive at the Laundromat. I ask for change, load my laundry, and hear them sighing behind me. Because I don't understand Spanish I have no idea what they are so upset about, but they seem very upset. So what is going on, Elena? I ask. The man, no good, she says.

And that is the end of her sentence.

Then I notice that the woman is carrying a long white cane. Is she blind? I ask. And I gesture blind, hands over the eyes.

Si si, Elena says, excited that I have understood, though I really haven't.

Sometimes I suggest that Elena and Ava watch an American soap to improve their English, but they have been in Nueva York for twenty-odd years and why am I trying to change them? Their lives were okay from my point of view until I met Elena on the street one day and she told me—in fractured, pidgin English—that she was looking for a new apartment –three bedroom (holding up three fingers)—four sons, (holding up four fingers), two high school dropouts, two working—one husband (holding up one finger) who comes to the Laundromat occasionally to help Elena load and fold. He speaks even less English than Elena, if that is possible, and works as a janitor at a bar downtown. How I figured this out I have no idea. I just kept asking questions. And, of course, my conclusions might be completely wrong.

A STORY ABOUT AN UNDULATING ROAD

She was walking down an undulating road. Once, only once, she turned around. She saw a small, brown-skinned child wearing an orange shirt. The shirt was very bright and fit the child perfectly. Behind the child was a tall, thin figure, and then another, and another, all equally spaced along the road. They felt like shadows of her former self, or her ancestors. Yes, perhaps they were her ancestors. In that case, the child was her descendant.

Ahead, the road was empty, shimmering in the bright summer light, not beckoning exactly, but open, like a ribbon unravelling into eternity.

Was it a procession, a pilgrimage, or a death march? They passed a farm, or what looked like a farm from her vantage on the road. It was to the right, surrounded by an electrified fence. There were signs: "Beware." She kept her distance and stopped. Strange animals romped around, playfully. Some looked like dinosaurs, others like overgrown hairy goats. They were having fun, it seemed, laughing, oblivious to the world outside the fence or their own eccentricity.

A STORY ABOUT FRIENDSHIP

How does one describe friendship? She is a good friend, we say, but what does that mean? She wasn't a good friend is easier. She didn't show up as promised, for example. Or she was a friend just for the season, or a reason. Of course, we don't realize that at the time, do we? When we begin a friendship, and then solidify it, we assume it will be for life because we expect to mate for life, like geese, and we expect, or at least I do, that friends are the same. But they appear and disappear. And so do I. Or, I move away. Or, it's just over and I hang on and hang on. Or I stop answering emails and phone calls. Really? That's awful, I tell myself. But I do it anyway.

So here's a story that illustrates my over-all disappointment in friendship as a human institution: A friend calls to say hello after a hiatus of several months. No reason for it; we live in the same town. Just busy, right? So how are you doing? Okay, and you? I answer with the usual platitudes without launching into anything specific. Then her voice shifts into another key. She has something to say and it's about us:

I've missed you, she says.

What? I say because I am really perplexed and don't know how to answer, so I say, I don't understand.

I've missed you. I trusted you. Where have you been? When you came to dinner to meet my son, you made promises.

I made promises?

Yes. You don't remember?

No.

I offered some tea and listened to her talk about her troubled son. I still couldn't remember any promises. I said I had to get back to work. She left and I washed the tea cups and that was that. The friendship was over.

A STORY ABOUT A SNAKE

You still recall the Sundays on the porch of your parents' summer house and the day the snake visited and your mother chased it with a broom. Speckled linoleum covered the floor, the perfect camouflage until the snake began to move. It smelled of earth and felled trees still fresh with sap. It opened its mouth and it hissed, its black-green skin, solid and unadorned, rippled on the cool floor. Then you remember the sting of anger and betrayal as you watched your mother lower the broom onto the snake's back. It could have been saved, you shouted over the high-pitched frightened voices of your parents' guests.

And the next morning it was still there. You picked it up with a child's shovel, walked it to the back of the property, and buried it.

WHEN I WAS AN AIRPLANE

I was on the tarmac waiting for take-off packed between one hundred planes and not one flying, but twenty waiting to descend, the first ten without fuel the others without food or water, disabled by endless travel, and I thought I was an epilated bird, too vulnerable to soar. Then, suddenly, lift-off and the clouds beneath me at 32,000 feet, the possibility of free-fall in every landing. I loved the cruising best, every flash of light from the retreating sun and darkness around the curved halo of the earth, no parachute under the seats, or life rafts, or oxygen masks, the emergency doors flung open, passengers ejected from their seats, arms thrashing, as they drifted to their destinations.

LOST

There are only two places in the United States where I get lost: Los Angeles and 601 West 26th Street in Manhattan. One morning on a recent visit to LA, I was staying in Sherman Oaks with some friends—that's in "the Valley"—and I went out for an early morning run. The sun had risen in the east, but I couldn't locate it exactly because everything was so bright. What I should have done is click the "where is my car, where am I" app on my phone, but I forgot, or didn't think of it. So I set out into what looked like an easy neighborhood to navigate—a flat, grid-like layout interrupted by long avenues leading who knows where? I stopped now and again to admire the vegetation—lush and exotic—and then I continued going this way and that, telling myself: no problem, I know where I am. And then, suddenly, I didn't know where I was and the street was empty. I was jet lagged, on New York time, and that made the confusion worse. I sat on some shallow stairs leading to a pretty stucco house—I love stucco—and sipped on my water bottle. I had my phone, I could call my friends, but I didn't want to wake them. Hmm. Are there any police cruising these streets, I wondered? Los Angeles is a city of cars, but there were no cars. Too early. Then I saw a stout woman approaching the intersection. A mirage? No, she was real. Stout, carrying packages, wobbling from side to side. She greeted me in Spanish and I attempted to do the same. Donde. Good thing I knew that word. And I told her the address. No speak English, she said, and off she went, to clean someone's house, or look after someone's children most probably. I waited a half hour. By then my friends would be up and wonder where I was, I hoped. I should have left a note, but hadn't thought of that either. I remembered the time I'd gotten lost at 601 West 26th street, a converted warehouse, huge, a city block nearly, where I had attended an event a few years back. The hallways were endless, the turnings a labyrinth, every doorway the same, and after I came out of the restroom, I couldn't find the elevator, everyone was gone, the halls deserted. Ultimately, I went down the staircase and found my way onto the street but I had been terrified, and remembered that terror, so I finally called my friends and said, "I'm having an Alice in Wonderland experience." They came to get me and walked me back, just around the corner.

GARGOYLES

She went to the waterfront late one afternoon to study the gargoyles. They were on the parapet of The Grand Hotel owned by an Indian businessman. The gargoyles arrived when he took over the hotel, one of many renovations. Before this, the parapet was just a parapet, the town of Victoria just a touristy seaside town. She had been born and raised in Victoria, she had married there, but had never visited The Grand Hotel, or its gargoyles.

She had heard about them at a party at the college where she worked. It was the dean, a former lover, who told her about them. "The gargoyles are grotesque," he had told her. "You will love them." How did he know this? She would wake and he would be beside her and she would turn towards him and, together, they discussed the underbelly of Victoria and their lives, a bonding. Too many lace curtains, they always agreed, in this very upright touristy seaside town.

And so, one afternoon, she set out to study the gargoyles. It was a pilgrimage, she thought, to seek out the ridiculous in our humdrum lives.

The front of the hotel faced the quay where the ferries docked. There was always a high wind there no matter the weather anywhere else. There were earthquakes sometimes, too, which whipped the wind and waves into frenzy. Nonetheless, it was well known that the population of Victoria always remained calm.

Observing the facade of the hotel, she noticed that the gargoyles' mouths were open. They were sucking air, growling and snarling. Their faces were bitter and vituperative. One of the gargoyles, set into the corner of the parapet, was devouring the sky.

She opened her palm-sized sketchbook and began to draw. Each gargoyle was slightly different. One had a long neck, the other a bulbous torso. She gave each of the gargoyles a name. She called the one devouring the sky "on the edge."

RECORDING A DINNER PARTY CONVERSATION

I'm preparing a dinner party and cuing up the recorder on my phone so that the conversation is documented. I am quite certain that the give and take between my erudite friends will be scintillating, as it usually is. We are all professors at the university complex in Abu Dhabi and our lives are hermetic. Dinner parties provide a welcome breather from the strain of working here on two and three year contracts.

At first, it all seemed like a great adventure, until the revelations. Now we don't know exactly where we are in this tainted universe of "globalization." What a word. Though no one has so far admitted the specter of uncertainty, there is great uncertainty.

It's my guess that Jalilah will be the first to broach the subject. She's the most politically astute and, because she's been a one-term policy wonk in Washington, we cleave to her assertions and evaluations. She's articulate and knowing; we all are. That's why we are here isn't it? The chosen ones, we call ourselves, in a self-deprecating way, of course.

I'll have to do something about the ambient noise as the microphone is very sensitive. No one will think it strange that my phone is on the table as we are always awaiting calls and texts from loved ones back home. The phone goes black even as it is recording so no one will know, or will they?

I hear my guests arriving. Excuse me while I put on the soup.

HIS HEAD IS AN ORANGE

His head is an orange. His glasses are yellow. His eyes are pink. His teeth are pits running across his cheeks like fire. When he smiles, which he does often, sweet juice comes out of his nostrils. He wears a pinwheel hat that spins gently in the wind. When he lopes onto the stage, the audience gasps, and then applauds. There is no doubt that he will win the election.

A STORY ABOUT A DEAF MUSICIAN

I went to the press conference to get the story. The most famous rock musician of the decade was deaf, the release said. Years ago, during a philanthropic mission to a war zone, he had witnessed the explosion of a land mine, and though he had been spared, the explosion had damaged his hearing, permanently.

The musician's handlers had kept the injury secret, and though some hearing returned in gradual increments, the musician had become tone deaf, and he could no longer decipher scales or keys. Melodies continued to effloresce inside him, but he could not release them onto the page. Nor could he play with his band any more. He had tried to mime, but this had become impossible also. He had stopped performing without explanation; now there was an explanation. In the studio, the technicians could compensate for the musician's difficulty by transposing his lyrics into sounds.

All this was explained at the press conference, and it was impressive, a good story. I listened carefully. I took notes. And then I walked home through the park. It was spring and there were many visitations: birds from Siberia, birds from Antarctica, tourists. I thought of the musician's plight, his invisible injuries. Not even his lover's words were audible to him.

HAIRY ARMS

Here I am swimming in the medium slow lane again, on my back to rest my back, and I am so close to the lane divider that I am touching the man with hairy arms in the fast lane whenever I am in the pull position with my left arm. This is really disgusting. I don't know how to avoid this unplanned touching because I have a wide stroke, my coach tells me, and I have to swim close to the edge of the lane. I want to stop and say hey, watch it, because he has a wide stroke too though he is on his stomach doing freestyle, pushing speed, doing flip turns, type A Daddyo, and never stops to apologize, or to find out if he's hurt me, though why should he? Bad luck, this guy swims at the exact same time I do. I can't wait to see him outside of the pool. In the elevator, for example. I have fantasies about this, the two of us in the elevator, alone. We get in at the same time and stand side by side. I look to my left and I don't recognize anything but his hairy arms. Do I say something? Remain quiet? Ask if he's had a good swim?

THE INTERVIEW

My source had told me a hippie was living in town. My editor wanted me to do an interview and snap a picture. What was it like to be a hippie back in the day? That was the hook, as we say.

He was homeless and, weather permitting, either slept on the beach or on a bench in the center of town, or down by the estuary. I had never seen him, and couldn't find him, at first, so I stopped a policeman I knew and asked where I could find this hippie. "Do you know where he is on any given day?" I thought that was a good question.

"Usually," the policeman said. "People complain even though he is quiet and doesn't bother anyone. I keep an eye. Give him some food now and again. In the winter he'll have to go into a shelter."

"I wonder how he ended up here?" I asked.

"Beats me," said the policeman.

This is an upscale town which has slowly been taken over by the 0.0.1%. I am not one of them and I don't even live here. I'm just a cub reporter trying to build a portfolio before I move on, hopefully into the big city. So I am always looking for interesting stories. There aren't many round here.

It was a mellow summer day and the hippie was down by the estuary splayed out on a bench. I smelled him before I saw him and, though his clothes looked clean enough, they were patched together. The water was in high tide, the gulls were screeching, and there was a lot of traffic coming over the bridge, not a congenial location for an interview. I stood in front of the hippie and asked if he'd like a cup of coffee and something to eat. He said, "sure," and we walked side by side over to Starbucks.

He was very tall with long braided hair and a whitening beard. His skin was leathery and he was wearing a vest. His chest was bare and hairy. He had colorful ornaments in his hair and around his neck. They were beautiful, obviously handmade, which he confirmed when I asked him as soon as we sat down with our drinks. He had ordered an herb tea and a scone; I had a strong coffee. I needed the coffee. Something about this man was unsettling, but what? He seemed sane, peaceful. What was wrong with him that he could live so freely and so apart? What was wrong with me that I was so disinterested?

"Have your coffee," the hippie said.
It was only then that I asked his name. It was Ed.

FIVE STRANGE THOUGHTS
NOT NECESSARILY RELATED

Note: The reader is free to change the order of these strange thoughts.

1. Frail old man. You don't know how much I love you.
2. I am raw flesh, serrated, moist, insensate. You lick my wound.
3. Life is a net: it catches living things.
4. This chair forgives my body. Soft, I sleep.
5. Has it ever occurred to you how many people we know?

3. FIAT LUX

A STORY ABOUT TWO BROTHERS TALKING IN A CAFÉ

Sometime in the middle of the afternoon as they were sitting in the cafe discussing politics, the two brothers heard thunder. Or they thought it was thunder. In retrospect, they understood that the rumbling sound was not thunder, it was the tanks massing outside the city. They continued talking, oblivious to the warning sounds. The strudel arrived, and then the coffee. One of the brothers—the younger—had ordered apple strudel, the other poppy seed. They always shared their strudels.

WEATHER REPORT

A man I know went for a walk on a country lane where he had just bought himself a weekend cottage. He had checked the weather report before setting out even though it was usually wrong. The cottage—albeit substantial and winterized—was in the mountains which has its own climate, a micro-climate; the weather is fickle there. But the man was an optimist and assumed an end of winter sun, ample in its warmth, and a benign breeze. The grasses alongside the road were beginning to regenerate and the mountains in the distance settled in a jagged configuration on the horizon line.

The man was a frugal, disciplined person, a financier in his city life, and he didn't like to dress more than once a day. If he had an appointment in the evening, he dressed for that appointment: creased trousers, a crisply ironed cotton shirt, leather shoes, and though he wasn't prepared for a country walk, he set out anyway and, once on his way, the weather report was confirmed. *It's accurate for once,* he thought. But what is beautiful from afar, or virtually through the lens of his cell phone, often becomes disfigured at close range. He hadn't noticed the clouds or taken them into consideration.

Suddenly it was raining, a driving rain, and the wind had come up so strongly he had to stop and hang on to the stump of tree. There were no houses in sight and no shelter; he was completely exposed to the elements. Within minutes, his jacket and clothes and shoes were drenched and he was afraid. *I have been hit by a tidal wave*, he thought. No cars passed and there was no cell phone coverage. He waited for the flash storm to subside before turning back to the house. By then it was dark and he had missed his appointment.

STAND FAST IN RUSHING WATER

One day in late summer, after a fierce storm, a man went fishing in the creek. The sky was still dark and the water was rushing past him, swirling into itself, devouring the bedrock, and throwing pebbles and debris onto the bank. But the man thought it was the right time to go fishing. He cast out his line and stood quietly on the bank of the rushing river. There was a sign tacked to a pylon of the bridge upriver, but it was too far away for him to see. TUBERS KEEP TO THE RIGHT. It was well known by the locals that there were dangers on this stretch of the river that worsened after a storm: jagged stones, eddies and sinkholes. The man was a local but this particular stretch of the river was not familiar to him, though he imagined he had been there before.

The fisherman walked north along the bank towards the bridge pulling his line behind him. It snagged on rocks, he lost his bait continually, but he persevered. He felt a bit chilled and began to fantasize sitting in front of a fire with a thick book. He missed his wife.

In the past, he had enjoyed the solitude of fishing, the thought of his family safely at home in a house he had built, expanded, and repaired lovingly over the years. But something had changed: the loss of his wife, his children and grandchildren all far away. Suddenly the solitude became something else: loneliness.

The man was so distracted by these troubling thoughts that he hadn't noticed the reel separating from his rod. It came undone and whipped backward, hitting him in the middle of his forehead. He fell to the ground, stunned. The rod and reel were gone, catapulting towards the waterfall a mile away. Only the red and white sinker remained, bobbing in the water by his left foot.

THE HMS LUSITANIA

I dreamt I was the captain of the Lusitania. It was 1915 and we were nearing the Irish coast when a U-boat surfaced just twenty-five yards to starboard. These facts are all wrong, of course, but that was my dream. And it continued: I saved the Lusitania. It did not sink. No one died.

This is a either a story about changing history or not accepting fate, or both. I refused to accept the great liner's fate. I stayed on the bridge when the torpedo hit—I was the Captain after all—and after a successful evacuation of all the passengers, I roamed the empty, smoldering deck. I admired the beauty of the portholes, the creak of the timber, the soft swell of the sea, and the salty lubricious spray where all life began.

After the bombardment, against all expectation, the ship remained seaworthy and level. Nonetheless, the evacuation was necessary. For the most part, it was orderly, but a few passengers were panic-struck and jumped to their certain deaths. So I am revising history again: not everyone survived. As for me, the last soul on board what turned out to be—ultimately , in another lifetime—a sinking ship, I was steadfast and serene. I watched the sunset and, the next morning, I watched the sunrise.

Throughout most of this ordeal, the offending U-boat remained at the bow of the ship. Then in the morning, like most nocturnal creatures, it departed silently. By evening of the second day after the attack, rescue ships arrived, and all but a few passengers returned safely to port, but I stayed aboard. Using the constellations and my intuition, I steered the wounded, limping ship to port.

IN TRANSIT

The railroad station was a hut in the middle of a forest, a way-station, as capacious as a barn, unheated, soiled. The floor was compressed sand, sifted and layered, like the silt at the bottom of the river, moist and dense with cadavers and ash.

A man and a woman sat on a bench and waited for the train. They had been walking for days, eating berries and ferns. The ferns were bitter and caught in their throat. The man spit. The woman choked and heaved. They had sent their children ahead with strangers more than a month ago.

They were hungry and embarrassed by their hunger. The woman wanted an apple. She had been dreaming of an apple. The man wanted bread and had been dreaming of bread. He was chewing on his tongue.

Her hair was blonde, her face wide. A friendly and open face, a smile without teeth from the months they had been on the road sleeping in shacks, scrounging for food, like wolves. The man was dark-haired, his eyes cerulean blue. He had been a handsome man, loved by many women, a loving, handsome man, a husband now.

The air was fetid and still, high summer. A desert in the midst of the forest, an abandoned train station. But the man and the woman did not notice its abandonment. They sat. They waited.

In ordinary times, it should not be difficult to locate a source of sustenance, a zone of safety, ones' children, a train.

TRACK 218

I've been to the train station before but not with strangers and they are all women and I have no luggage and by accident I've brought the broken red shopping cart but it's empty. I stand in line at a series of information booths. All the men behind the windows are in uniform.

They are patient with my inquiries. Where? How? They hand me printed cards with track numbers and tablets with routes etched on touchstone screens. Where is the red cart? I could use it now. My hair parts and turns silky so I take selfie pictures and record sounds on the platform—the air, the smoke and, in my left ear, someone whispering: Track 218. Track 218.

THE SIEGE

It begins early in the morning. First, the gathering of troops on the parade ground, then the drill, preparations for an anticipated skirmish. Is a skirmish the same as a battle? Has the battlefield shifted?

Later, they set out on forested roads. It was winter. The soldiers—all so young—were wearing snowflakes on their ears, pajamas, and thin socks. They had been torn out of bed for an exercise, a maneuver, they had been told. But they lost their way and staggered behind enemy lines into bloodied terrain where corpses of the enemy lay decaying in the road and on the side of the road. That is when the barrage started.

A soldier turned his head to admire a waterfall and weeping willows, the landscape of his youth, he said. Another started humming a tune and began to dance.

WAR ZONE

The sound of jets roused her from sleep. Outside, the still wintry overcast sky lay speckled and worn. Now there were navy blue fighter jets overhead in re-configured flight path. They approached and then veered away, their engines thrumming and spewing fumes. She watched with incredulity as one plane spun downward nose first into the settlement of houses just yards away from her windows. Only poor people lived there and it was as though they had been targeted by the machines designated to protect them, those enormous navy blue planes with white markings and red lettering. Eerily, there was no sound or smoke as the buildings swallowed the plane's body and then its tail. All was in stasis until hysteria and then motion erupted. Ambulances arrived. In the distance, a woman with curly black hair was sunbathing on a sand dune, oblivious and inured. It's a scene she'd witnessed before: Sevastopol after the Liberation, that famous photograph from May, 1944, men and women in the rubble of a shattered city catching the sun, and smiling.

INTO THE MOUNTAINS

It was cold and dark, the dead of night, past curfew, as we approached our house. The war was nearly over, but there was still danger. Resistance fighters were tunneling through the mountains into the villages and taking them over. So we were fearful and remained vigilant.

Sometimes, however, life went on as if it were normal, or perhaps we had become accustomed to pretending that it was normal. That night, we had gone to visit friends and Joaquim had challenged Peter to a game of chess. I stayed in the kitchen talking to Louise, as women do. We were both grateful we didn't have children to protect during the horrible, long war, but wanted to start a family soon. Suddenly it was late and we had a discussion about whether we should stay or leave. I don't know why we made a reckless decision. I could sense trouble; my intuition was never wrong. And when we arrived at the house, we saw a light. Unwanted guests—the fighters—were helping themselves to our supplies.

We scurried down the path like ferrets. We were animals now, so the analogy came easily. In and out of hedge grows, head down, arms swinging wildly, running and running until the sun came up. Occasionally we stopped and turned over rocks to search for worms, a source of protein, and also fennel. Fennel, with its biting licorice flavor, had become our favorite food.

The soldier who captured us was from my village. We had gone to school together. He was wearing a navy blue coat, army issue, and a powder blue woolen cap that matched his eyes. His face had aged, the once smooth skin was now rutted with experience. Cigarettes had roughened his voice. He was no longer insouciant, he was grave. He reminded me of an actor I had once admired.

I stepped forward and reached out for him. Perhaps if we could touch, I thought. But his pistol was pointed at Joaquim's heart and then it was pointed at my heart.

We began our silent ascent into the mountains. The trail was narrow. Tall grass spires swished over us with a rush of air. A small deer crossed our path and began grazing a berry patch. Soon it was night again. The soldier's flashlight illuminated the path, and then the cave. Was that a smile? I wasn't certain.

The cave was a safe haven where we could rest and talk, the soldier said. After that, our fate was not in his hands.

THE CAVE

They lived in a cave in the mountains. It was well furnished. The ground was mined, but this was of no consequence as they had purchased special shoes. These shoes detected mines within a six foot circumference. One foot slowly in front of the other foot. Progress was slow, but this also was of no consequence. Because they had no place to go, each day had become predictable.

In the morning they searched for food and water, berries and leaves. Their digestion had reverted to this vegetarian diet. They followed the bears' spoor which guaranteed a meal by midday. Their stomachs rumbled as they remained focused on their task. They had no words to explain their feral existence.

There were other caves in proximity, all well furnished. Clusters of men, women and children. They might once have been relations or neighbors, but this, also, was of no consequence. As an observer, one would say they were people of disparate and unknown association. They had re-formed themselves. They had no history.

TO FLEE (A VERB)

Taking some things I want. Leaving some things I'll never want. Taking some things I think I'll want. Leaving some things I thought I'd want. Taking some things I'll never need. Taking some things I'll always need. Taking some things to store. Leaving some things forevermore.

THE ANT FARM

She was reading about ants in a novel. Why were the ants there? She stepped inside the protagonist's head and tried to figure it out. Oh frabjous day! Within minutes she saw what the characters saw and felt what they felt: revulsion. Though miniscule, the ants were grotesque. A lab technician—one of the characters in the story—removed glass from one of the tanks and explained that ants never tried to escape. They existed to service the regal few: a Queen, her Consort, the Courtiers. This biological arrangement was aesthetically pleasing to scientists, apparently. Then, a few paragraphs later, the ants worked frenetically to dismember a captured scorpion. She stopped reading; this was too much. But the next morning on the way to work, she began reading again. Why did she find the story so compelling? The diorama of the ant farm—two dimensional on the page—had become three dimensional in her head: the ants, their society, thescorpion, the lab technician. Pure evil in an unquestioning world.

MY MOTHER IS AN OLD TREE

My mother is an old tree. My mother is a felled tree behind the house. My mother burns. My mother did not always love her life or us. My mother carried her murdered mother onto the porch. My mother killed the soldier with a spoon.

A STORY ABOUT A FARMER IN WARTIME

A farmer was standing on his porch at sunrise. Slicers rained down from the sky and erupted in his fields. Several landed close to the house, sparked, and ignited the dry grass. The fire smoldered and shifted direction, sparing the house.

The farmer thought, "I have to feed my family. I have to plow in some seeds. It will be summer soon." It was as if he didn't see the fire that was surrounding the house. Perhaps he was in a daydream that carried him somewhere else, his idyllic childhood, or his vacation in Sicily when he had turned twenty. Now he was forty—too old to be conscripted, too young to succumb to despair.

A whooshing sound in the distance brought him out of his daydream, the grasslands in the distance burned and the man remained on the porch and thought. He heard his wife and children screaming, and then they were silent, and he knew they were gone.

He walked into the barn and pulled out a burlap bag of alfalfa seed. He walked into a field and tossed the seeds into the still unfertilized furrows.

He remembered his parents and how they had encouraged him. "You have a good head on your shoulders," his father had always said. His teachers agreed. But they were all dead now—his parents, his teachers—living only in his memory. It was strange how he could always conjure them in the field as he was tossing seed. Why had they not prepared him for this war?

He was decapitated in an instant. His head fell into the furrow, the marigold eyes startled open. The headless torso sank to its knees, remaining upright like a groundhog feeding on a nut, or a congregant at prayer.

Within days the seeds had sprouted in the furrows. But no one was there to harvest them.

THE OUTCASTS

Once upon a time a man, an outcast, lived inside the crater of an inactive volcano. His skin was scarred by whippings. He had such outlandish thoughts that even his parents did not want to hear them when he was a boy. It was they who had sent him to live inside the volcano, exiled like Cicero had been exiled from Rome. In fact, Cicero was also living inside the volcano and the two men were companions of sorts; they helped each other survive hardships, sharing food and scrap timber for fires and shelter.

Underneath the volcano's footprint was a lake of ice though this was not known to the two outcasts for a long time. The volcano was only temporarily inactive, it was coming to life again, and the ice was melting. But one starry night the gurgling sound of the water alerted them and they began their trek across the valley, out of exile, and down into the valley where life had continued happily without them. The lava was slippery and the men lost their grip from time to time, but they leaned into the mountain and kept going, conversing at length and shouting encouragement to each other. Soon they were in a village which, to their surprise, was empty of human habitation.

OCCUPIED

The room is cluttered when she arrives, and there is a vinegary smell. A natural cure for cockroaches, she heard someone say. Pour vinegar into the cracks, let it evaporate at its own speed. Is she evaporating? She takes off her Gortex jacket, folds it neatly, and places it mindfully on the bed. Grey army issue wool blanket. She's noting all the details. Her mind is occupied. *How long will I stay? Where are my books? Where are my clothes?* If only she could ask these questions. If only someone could answer them. But the door is shut, she is alone, and the corridor is silent. The room is illuminated by one light bulb hanging on a wire. *I am empty handed. I have no belongings.* This is where her thoughts stop. She sits on the bed next to her jacket. *The past is baggage enough, if only I could make use of it.* She walks to the window and contemplates the vista. Mountains in the distance, fields touching the brick wall, shacks and barns. All in the present tense. Dogs, horses, ploughs, a well in the center of the village.

AFTER THE SLAUGHTER
Inspired by Caspar Friedrich

After the battle, he ran into the woods. Now he was watching the soldiers from behind the bushes, three men dressed in capes and hats, their masks discarded and lying on the fallow ground, out of time or, perhaps, of this time. They were conversing intently, though he was too far away to hear their words clearly. Two of the men had bloodied brows, the other a bloodied hand. The landscape, once so marvelous and true, was tainted, the hill falling away under the soles of their muddied shoes. The sky darkened, a gibbous moon, a star, the funnel of the universe collapsing and then expanding above them. He moved closer and heard them say—clearly suddenly—that they would return to kill, the battle was half won and only half over, they would destroy the village, slaughter all that remained alive. He thought of his family—all gone—his friends—all gone—and the layby on the side of the road where he had first made love.

BIBLICAL VOICES

Yet another eyeless day in Gaza, yet another marriage in an orchard on a hill, yet another sandstorm predicted and, in the final stanza, promises of redemption and ripened plums. In the distance, unknown fallen soldiers wrapped in linen reiterate prophecies. Closer still, jails over-run with vermin and lice, abandoned moonlit vistas, the crevice widening as an invalid nation retreats lamely to its rest. And, finally, Angels float on the surface of the Red Sea as herons stalk ancient mosaics.

THE ARTIFICIAL GARDEN

We retreated to the dead side of the planet as we had been instructed. It was a celluloid environment encased in lead. There was no escape.

We began to run but the air was so thin we choked. Child beggars were crawling along the edges of this world and the next. We boarded a monorail. Brahmins with oversized suitcases told us they were escaping into the hills. The monorail rocked, the earth heaved. There was no outside, only inside. Inch by inch, year by year, within our lifetime, we had moved closer to the sun. Warnings abounded, all unheeded.

My lover was soft and there was no heft to his flesh, no gravitas, and I was eroded, broken. I held my lover's hand and pulled him along, but even this tenderness could not save us.

Finally, we arrived at the artificial garden but Adam and Eve had fled.

FIVE THOUSAND YEARS
for Liat

Bombs are falling in Gaza, rockets are flying near Haifa. Birds that were twittering are now silent, or dead. They no longer greet the morning.

A man on the corner is begging for food. An unhappy woman is working in a bank. Children are playing games in the rubble.

No one thinks, why are we here? What is our purpose on earth? Why are we destroying ourselves and each other?

Five Thousand Years and all wisdom has fled. To love or fight? To cherish life or end it?

CHILDREN TO LOVE
*for the children of Gaza, Israel, Iraq,
Syria, Congo & Afghanistan*

These children I love, because they are children, I love them. That girl, that boy, a safe haven somewhere. All the trees had been felled, the earth was barren behind the house, but the children played, and their games continued, and belonged to them.

I had brought them all a gift and handed it to the girl. She unwrapped it slowly, its paper and ribbon dangling onto the floor, nearly tripping her as she walked away from me towards her friends and said, "Thank you for this gift." She spoke clearly in a universal language though she was very small. How old was she? Three? Four? I can hardly remember now.

We had escaped the bombing, a temporary reprieve. Rockets and mortars stored in underground tunnels and caves surfaced sporadically, yet the children continued playing, and whenever the adults gathered, it was an occasion. There was music, a bit of dancing, food. We told stories, we made love, we slept.

And we loved the children and gave them small gifts. We owned nothing. We possessed nothing. Only the children mattered.

PORTRAIT OF AN AID WORKER

She is wearing leather sandals and a black dress that grazes her ankles. Her blouse is pulled tight in a crisscross around her bosom. Most notable, there is a large coin hanging around her neck on a tong. Her deceased husband bought her this talisman in a market in South Sudan.

"How can money be purchased?" the reporter asks.

She takes out a box of cigarettes, lights one, and inhales deeply.

"I am surprised you smoke," the reporter says.

"I have been out of the country for twenty years," she says. "I've never seen The Sopranos. My clothes are out of fashion."

She gets up to leave, hugging a folder to her chest. Fully extended, it is now evident she is small in stature, diminished by the atrocities she has witnessed in the camps.

THE FOREST
for all the children

Welcome to the dark forest with its mushroom lacquered stumps. Up above, a canopy of leaves dense with summer light. Below, a stream running wild over eroded rocks, a purple cloth caught on a barnacled root, pebbles saturated with color. We paint our faces red, green, and blue, the sun hissing above us, insects feeding on our flesh.

Did you know that fish squat in the water waiting for bait, that they will do this even after we are gone? Therefore, tell me: What will save our world? What will open the hearts of warriors? Rockets or trees?

ONCE A GREAT NATION

Morning news report: The airport has been evacuated. I had a walkie-talkie on the seat beside me and shouted into it: "I'm in the parking lot. There are no cars. I am the only one here."

A voice answered: "I am in the café. I will wait for you."

I circled the parking lot several times but could not decide on the right spot and stopped. The engine idled.

The sky was gray, the clouds moving swiftly across the abandoned runways. Gulls feasted on the debris of rotting in-flight dinners, their plastic wrappings torn open.

The walkie-talkie crackled. "I am still waiting for you," the voice said.

I did not answer. I drove around the empty parking lot one last time before exiting the airport.

There were no cars on the road, no planes in the sky, and the bridge I'd taken just an hour ago had shattered.

GREAT DELICACIES

A long-married American couple were having dinner in an inn in Japan high in the mountains. It was a small inn and they were the only guests. The air was moist and clear. Words dripped easily and the man and the woman, celebrating their 20th wedding anniversary, were content.

A live fish was brought to the table, a great delicacy, they had read. The fish was speared in the middle with a wooden stick. It blinked knowingly.
The woman said, "I won't be able to eat this fish."

The man said, "We will insult the innkeeper if we do not eat this fish."

Several minutes had passed. The innkeeper came to their table to ask, in halting English, if everything was alright. The man tried to explain that though they knew the fish was a great delicacy, a gift from the innkeeper, they would not be able to eat the fish.

"We would like some rice," the woman said, miming eating rice with her chopsticks.

The innkeeper went into the kitchen to get some rice. He said to his wife, who was the cook, "These Americans will not eat the fish." Then they both laughed.

During the occupation, the inn had been closed for a while, but then it re-opened. American soldiers came to visit often and they were rude and condescending to the innkeeper and his wife. This is when they decided to change the menu to "great delicacies." The live fish was a favorite among the soldiers.

NOMADS

I'm writing these words lying on my left side on a freshly made bed. The sheets are off-white, a cream color. My tongue is resting on my teeth. The window is open and there is a fresh breeze off the water. Boats, fishermen, a child running naked on the beach, wafting smell of spices cooking.

I'm lying quietly, drifting in and out of sleep. The journey was arduous, a lot of tumult, constant danger. Now, finally, a respite.

Have I mentioned the desert crossing? Day and night we walked the dunes bypassing the crevasses of history, or so we thought. Long-ago stars flickered as we darted through the dry landscape.

We seek shelter from the chaos, dragging once again into exile. Maybe this time we'll stay awhile, we'll rest awhile.

THE WEEK OF POSITIVE THINKING

I thought I'd write a story about the new puppy in our family who has amber eyes with green trim, a delicate head with droopy ears and chocolate fur. That would have been story enough as she is completely adorable and we are all in love with her. But then there was a knock on the door, the farmer across the road delivering logs for our wood stove. We stepped outside onto the pine needle carpet dusted with snow and there it was: a pileated woodpecker more than a foot long. All the ornithologists had thought it was extinct. They were wrong. I take a moment to think about this. I sip my tea. I ignore the newspaper with its dire warnings and when I do open it I try to pay attention to the good news buried somewhere on page 10, but the print is so small, it barely exists, so I decide to write my own headlines: OUR NEW PUPPY ARRIVES. THE PILEATED WOODPECKER RETURNS.

IDEA FOR A KIDNAPPING RESCUE

At the beginning of the week, there was news about the smart girls kidnapped in Nigeria. There were demonstrations in many cities and many countries. Very large nations contemplated sending soldiers to find the girls, but this never happened. Why didn't it happen? The girls had been captured *en masse*, more than 200 of them.

It might help, I thought, if we all sang a song once a day in honor of these lost girls, perhaps in the morning before breakfast, or when we are showering, or combing out our hair in our tutti frutti rooms with full length mirrors and plants on the windowsills.

Every kidnapped girl has an empty room; she is no longer there. The room is a clean slate, all history erased, a new beginning, a fresh start, where a child can be a child again, positive and hopeful, and free of a cruel fate such as kidnapping.

Sunlight is streaming through bubbled windows. Time slips. The girls are here, as before, tucked into their beds for the night.

4. MUSA

THE ARTIST AND HIS MUSE
inspired by a de Kooning painting

Recently, an artist told me about a model he destroyed with his brush. She did not realize his intention so continued to pose for him, day after day, week after week. He paid her well, or well enough, he told me. And she was flattered by his interest and attention. "I understood her from the inside out and the outside in," he boasted. "I could sense her moods and posed her accordingly."

One day the model arrived on a bicycle. It had been a gift from her grown son who thought she would enjoy the exercise and freedom. She lived about two miles away from the artist and was reliant on a tram which didn't run very frequently. The artist was often angry at these unforeseen delays and was therefore pleased about the bicycle. "But she soon smashed it," the artist said. "The frame was twisted around her torso, bruising her limbs and imprisoning her spirit."

Even as she recovered, the woman came to pose for the artist, though travel was even more difficult for her. She understood that the consequences of a failed experiment were grave and she did not want to fail. The artist drew her with care, and she responded with devotion. But her body was now distorted and she walked with a limp. After several months, the artist began to loathe her. He drew her heart pulsing, her breasts pumping, and her flesh burning. Because he could no longer idealize her as a great beauty, he destroyed her. Hands, face, torso, breasts, and feet flowed like lava onto the artist's sandaled feet.

THE MUSE

She sat at her desk not knowing how to begin. She read a poem hoping the poem would stir a beginning. The poem did not stir a beginning.

Her muse had fled in the night. All that was precious and luminous had fled. All that was precious and luminous had been stolen and she was like a blind woman, her fingers tracing the nuanced lines on the surface of a stone, as friable as plaster, as soft as sponge.

She was bereft. The muse was her lover, the lover was her muse. Now she could feel her dreams but not remember them. They too had fled, or evaporated. Where does a dream go when it cannot be remembered?

She sat at her desk and said, *I will imagine*. She imagined an embrace and then a kitchen exuding the odor of garlic and wine, a cacophony of voices, pots, and stories. The muse came to life. The muse spoke.

PISSARRO AT AN EASEL IN POINTOISE

Scent of mint rising from the river, fish playing between the children's toes, nearly lunchtime. Wind in trees rushing into clouds, clouds efflorescing across the sky, sky pulsing into stars, stars becoming endless night, night looping back to day, earth rotating potatoes on a spit, chicken cooking with onions and herbs, inspiration of appetites.

I only see shapes, I only see color, I only see light, I scrape the landscape with my palette knife.

THE DREAM REPORTER

I have always believed that there is an argument to be made for tracking dreams, to be a reporter of dreams. The argument is conventional, that is to say, based on convention. But at what point, I am asking, does innovation become convention? And at what point are we obligated to disregard convention and to challenge the dream reporter?

Tracking dreams is an exercise in awareness and self-discovery, we are told. But what if the dream reporter is an informant? What then?

For example, though the dream reporter does not use electronic devices, he listens attentively and appears empathic. He shakes his head. His words are kind. He professes understanding, even compassion. And he is proceeding with the task of tracking dreams with what he perceives to be our implied permission. The dreams are there to be tracked so he will track them. Then, at the moment of reporting the dream to the public, he reveals our deepest and most strange fantasies. So is he friend or foe? Innovator or protector of the status quo?

There is an artifact known as the dream catcher. This is available to the dream reporter, if he chooses to make use of it. He usually does. Let the record show that the dream catcher was devised by Native people many eons ago as a sacred object. It is built like a spider's web and woven with feathers. And now it has been commandeered by the contemporary dream reporter for a different and more sinister purpose. The purpose is not unlike a credit check. Find out what the person applying for a loan has in the bank.

Find out what the dream catcher has caught of the dreamer's dreams.

It is a mistake to assume the dream reporter has a magical temperament or magical abilities. He is simply an employee of the state who has been trained at the taxpayer's expense.

DREAMS

Poets have written about the country of dreams. In this country there are familiar roads and pleasant laybys, but also vectors, elisions and chasms. The sun sets as expected, or not. At times, the earth refuses to turn, or when it turns, the meadows bloom.

The dream may signify utopia or dystopia. Naked children play, or drown. A gray-haired man in a tweed suit sits alone at a table in an expensive restaurant, his face illuminated by candlelight. A woman goes into labor and weeps, or laughs.

FOUR

A story of four paragraphs, four lines each. There were always four of them. Four sets of eyes, four voices, four seasons, four cups, four saucers, four recorded conversations, one leading to another until the conversation stopped and the story ended. There could not be a fifth because the fifth did not exist. And if it did exist, he could not find it.

And then there are images, repeated four times. Open sun roofs, windy days, oceans and, in the distance, wheat fields and barns. The world is symmetrical, two on each side, two hemispheres, two nations, two hundred million people, four hundred million all together, a planet with four moons, all shining brightly.

He is grateful that the story of four can speak, that he is able to receive it. Its' tender words, an open sun roof, wind tossing his hair, the smell of manure, the sound of birds, a dog barking, a tractor. The story ends. The fifth line and the fifth paragraph remain invisible. He has arrived at the end of the story of four in four paragraphs.

THE WHITE DRESS
after a painting by Thomas Wilmer Dewing

Inside a golden frame, inside a sunlit room, glowing with affection, two women are facing the sea, one in a chair, naked, head bowed, the other in a long white dress, the hem green with algae. The naked woman steps onto the horizon and then out of the frame. Then the sun shifts and there are ghostly reflections, chimères, the Haitians call them. In the distance, the ocean beats back the future while, inside the room, the rod iron chairs set at angles in the sand remain fixed, until the dunes collapse.

READING TO AN EMPTY ROOM

I just found out I'd be reading a poem in a famous café downtown. That is, I've been asked to read a poem I have not as yet written. Had I written the poem, I could prepare for the reading.

A man called to invite me to read. I was in the park gardening that day, planting bulbs and raking leaves, my Saturday occupation. The park is pure poetry, I always say. And I was in the park, in the midst of pure poetry, when my cell phone vibrated.

I put down the rake and moved away from the other gardeners. The caller had a low voice and, at first, I thought it was my husband, that there was some emergency, but he would not have disturbed my day if there was no emergency, and the number that came up was not known to me.

Your submission, the man said without introducing himself, I like it very much. What had I sent him? Who was he? From what journal? I'd like you to read, he said. Not this poem necessarily, but one or two others. A work in progress is fine.

The sensation of the empty room began. It's dark in the room and it smells of beer and burning candles, but there is no one there. I am at the podium facing an empty room. I clap my hands. Bravo, I say, and wait patiently for more applause, accolades so silent only I can hear them.

5. AMORE

GENERIC LETTER TO A LOVER FAR AWAY #1

Dear_____,

I am back in the city after a full summer away. In the country, I dreamt of car horns and rain. In the city I dream of birds and rain. In either place there is a magnet riveting us to the center of the earth. I wonder if you know this. Quite frankly _____, you live without awareness of the sensory delights of our environment. City or country you are oblivious. But let me not berate you. Let me continue with my discussion of country vs. city.

For example, the birds flock to their destination without reading maps or relying on GPS. They follow an unknown path—unknown to us, at least. This path is mythic, a labyrinth. Am I making sense? In the pond—remember the pond?—we swam with toads and salamanders. You were horrified and had your warts removed attributing them to the toads. So now your skin is smoother than mine.

This summer, without you, I rested on the pine needles. The needles were sharp and cut into my flesh. Did I mention I was splayed like a deer after a kill? Open, remorseful, unrequited. Did I mention I was innocent?

I remain,

Very sincerely yours,

_____

MEXICO

When I was in love, I sat in the front seat of the car. And when I fell out of love, I sat behind the driver, my head against the glass partition. The road and my memory of love drifted away.

When I was in love and we arrived at the farm where my husband was born and raised, I played with the donkeys in the corral. And when he took the journey north, and I fell out of love, and I went to the farm where he was born and raised to stay with his family, I ate vanilla ice cream cones with his sister's children. Tumbleweeds whirled in a dusty wind darkening the sky.

He is north of the border and I am in Mexico waiting for him. I have no children and I am out of love. Many years have passed, many days. The sun rises every morning and I have put out feeders for the birds and planted my garden.

THE BRIDE WORE WHITE

The bride wore white though the dress was plain satin without ruffles or decoration. A plain white dress with a straight across-the-breast bodice and a straight across-the-hips skirt with a slight bustle in the back, an echo of the distended stomach and, in its own way, a disguise.

The guests were waiting around the four poster bed. The posts were a dark oak, the bed all white, like the bride and her dress. The bed cover was plain, without flounces.

The bride entered stage left. The bride, the guests, the four poster bed, the white satin dress, the distended stomach with the quickening child kicking impatiently against the bride's diaphragm. The guests saw the kick and then heard a small voice say, "If you are searching for a bit of news, here I am."

What century are we in? Had the fetus already been to broadcast school?

Silently, the guests observed the bride. Her tresses, long and thick, framed her masked face. The mask was skin tight, sucked into the flesh of her face, every pore saturated with white-out. Only her lashes and red cupid lips surfaced in three dimension. "She doesn't want to be identified," someone murmured. It was one of the guests, an old man standing serenely against the wall, separate from the others, but also one of them.

Then the groom arrived. Descriptions of him abound, available in myths. He was a Prince Charming, a man of every woman's dreams, and so on. There is no need to repeat all these stories here. Suffice to say that the bride turned to find him standing at her back. She jumped into his arms and wrapped her legs around his torso, capturing him for all eternity. In one dramatic and chivalrous gesture, the groom ripped the mask from the bride's face as the guests sighed.

ONLINE DATING

We are sitting side by side in a darkened movie theater. The previews are about to begin. *If only he would touch me.* It is our third date and I can't concentrate. He'll probably want to talk about the plot, right? And I can't concentrate. It's not even that he's so attractive, at least not to me. I wonder if he's feeling the same, in reverse?

I sit up a bit straighter in my seat and feel a pimple on my back rub against my blouse. What if he undresses me? Should I warn him beforehand? *I have a pimple on my back. There is a run in my panty hose. My bladder is full.*

He eats his popcorn without offering me a morsel. That was a test when he asked me if I wanted my own popcorn. I said no, but I meant yes, because I wanted to share his popcorn and eat out of the same container. I thought that might be intimate. But he hasn't offered me a morsel. In between bites, he either puts the container on the floor, or on the empty seat next to him.

My fingers are twitching like they did when I was a child and my mother told me I was doing something wrong. I try to concentrate on the opening scenes of the movie. I put my elbow on the arm of his chair hoping he'll take my hand. But he doesn't take my hand.

WHY?

Why do I enjoy both solitude and crowds? And why is it so
humid today? Why do animals and flowers please me more
than people? Why do my friends beat me at Scrabble most of
the time? Why does it matter? Why would anyone announce
on FB that they are feeling poorly because of such and such
and such and such and expect instantaneous sympathy?
Why is it a relief when jury duty is over and you will never
be called again because in six years you will be over 75?
Why is that happy news and not grim news? Why is Chris,
the lifeguard, still so huge he can hardly get onto the chair?
Why did an oversized woman sit next to me on the bus and
think it was insulting when I moved away? Why did she give
me a dirty look, make a rude remark, and say something out
loud to her friend about my rudeness? Why don't I care that
a friend is mad at me and sending me anguished emails
about herself and her situation? Why is a stranger on the bus
talking about her love life on her cell phone so loud
everyone can hear her? Why doesn't she care that we all can
hear her? Why doesn't she let the guy go?

THE MAN WHO HAD A BABY

Once upon a time, a man had a baby. He called to say he was delivering the baby, that it was coming out slow and easy and he wasn't in any pain. I don't know why women complain, he said, this doesn't hurt at all.

Men don't have pain when they deliver babies, I thought. Well, bravo.

When I arrived at the man's house he was standing up making phone calls to more friends and asking them to come over to see the new baby that he had delivered so painlessly. He was wearing a tall Stetson hat cocked back on his head and cowboy boots and spurs.

When he finally put down the phone he was even more energetic and cheerful. I love babies, he said. I really love babies. The birth of this baby was a breeze. I am going to have more babies.

Then I looked around for the baby but it was nowhere to be seen. Where is the baby, I want to see the baby, I came over to see the baby, I said. How did you manage to have a baby?

New technology has made it all possible, he said. My store of choice is on Fifth Avenue just south of St. Patrick's Cathedral. The midwife was wonderful. Let me give you her card. Within an hour you can have a baby. You can choose your baby and then have her designed in your image—hair, eyes, skin color. The delivery, as I have said, is painless. Completely painless.

GENERIC LETTER TO A LOVER FAR AWAY #2

Dear_____,

So I am feeling a little peek-ed this morning as the Brits would say. I have seen you on FB—mutual friends—at a birthday picnic party in _____'s back yard, red and white checkered tablecloths, a band playing (it was a video no less), and to say I was not invited is an understatement; it is as though I don't exist. Whose lover are you? Everyone's always or no one's never?

Though it is summer, I note that you are dressed in wool and sitting arm in arm with a back I do not recognize, elbows and shoulders touching. Please state the obvious, *sotto voce* if you must, and confirm my observation: there are sea grasses seeding, but not in your back yard, only mine. Fecundity.

So, you are not telling again. Okay, I will recline in the hammock on our once happy porch and rest. But you should know by now that continuing silence will... what? Contain me.

Yours once again ever so sincerely,

I remain,

_____

DIORAMA

One again she had a dream about the man in the Brooks Brothers shirt. He was an angel, pale and wiry, barely visible against the bright background of the field in which they stood. The scene was a living diorama, but this was an oxymoron. A diorama is not living, it is dead.

The man was leaning against a tree and the woman was standing next to him. The sun was high and bright—controlled weather conditions—and the moon was visible in the eastern sky.

It wasn't complicated. It was easy to understand: The man and the woman looked through the glass into the darkened exhibition hall. Observers stopped to stare at them. Their bodies touched, but only ethereally. The crowd murmured.

He was an angel, woven of gossamer thread, his shirt—purchased and therefore known—was the only emblem of the real world beyond the diorama. If she moved, the diorama would be destroyed. If she tried to lean closer, the man would fall over and melt. She would melt. All that would remain of him would be the Brooks Brothers shirt. All that would remain of her would be the memory of the shirt.

AT THE COUNTRY CLUB

It was sunny, a summer sunny day, humid. They were sitting at the shallow end of the pool at an upscale country club. Life was sweet, they always said. They had no complaints.

They were both dressed in white halter top bathing suits, wrap-around batik lounge skirts and designer sun glasses, sexy well manicured women in their 40's. Married, two children each, all in day camp, husbands in the city working.

A waiter came by and took their order: iced green tea. "Let us add more cold to this day," one of the women said. "I am cold enough," said the other. This was a coded comment about her lover. It disturbed her friend's repose. "What do you mean?" she asked.

"I dream of him while he dreams of others," she said.

She spoke slowly, the words jammed in her throat. Her eyes were vacant behind her glasses.

GENERIC LETTER TO A LOVER FAR AWAY #3

Hello my love,

Time has passed and your voice has faded to a tattoo inside me. Slumbering one moment, alert the next, I become animated by a sentence, a word, or a breeze. Some say I am not permitted to this sensation of the tattoo or to hum your favorite tune in an effort to evoke you. Your voice: a harp inside a bell. The bell: clanging.

I might be walking along the street peacefully when I hear you, smooth as velvet. Though unexpected, you are welcome and I want you to stay.

I have heard through various vines that you are a continent away. Thus the miracle of our continuing intimate connection.

Have I mentioned that I erased all the photographs of you from my phone? This was rash and I am now doubtful of regret. Can you please send me a replacement or two forthwith.

Sincerely, I remain...

_____

THE LOOSENED WHEEL

When the car snapped open on the rutted roadway over the tide-driven river, brackish water flooded the cabin. She tried to mount the wheel as she gasped for air but it had come loose from its moorings. The sun glared and then sank into the horizon.

Hours later when the emergency vehicles arrived, they found her body clinging to the top of the car which had been carried onto the embankment. She almost made it, the workers all said. She was strong, persevering, but had lost her traction.

CERTAINTY WAS HER MANTRA

Once upon a time she knew exactly what to do and how to do it, what to say and how to say it. Certainty was her mantra. Her opinion mattered more than any other, she decided. She made enemies but she didn't care; she was indifferent, care-less (she could care less). She lived her life according to her own drummer, her friends and colleagues said. Invitations to dinner parties ceased. She's insufferable everyone agreed. Had she noticed? Yes and no.

In the summer, she escaped the hot city, and packed her still definitive certainties in a case with all her other summer belongings. She was certain that she was happy, for example. She was certain that the summer would be productive. Productivity was important to her. Goals. And in the past, this had been her happiness: her work. It took up a large space among her belongings: electronic equipment, folders, books, her academic reputation. But when she started to unpack the morning after her arrival at the bungalow, uncertainty overwhelmed her. She sat down on the floor and cried. She lost her appetite. She lost her certainty about the future, hers and others. Would there be no end to wars? Was there anyone she could call?

There was a thunderstorm that night and it frightened her. In the morning, it was still raining lightly and the birds twittered. She prepared the hummingbird feeders and went behind the house to pick wildflowers.

JUNK

One day, rummaging through the garage, he found a folder with his name on it. All the contents were new to him, a piece of his sequestered history.

He didn't have much energy that day—a sleepless night, too many obligations—and the thought of revelations after so much time had passed was not welcome. But the folder was there, an accusation: *Own up.* Because, in truth, he knew what was in it, had always known. Once the folder was open, he would not be able to continue the charade of anger.

He picked up the folder and opened it. It felt alive, animate. It was a decree authored by a judge when he was six years old: *Supreme Court, State of Maine.* His father's name, his stepfather's name, the word adoption, the word denied, the word final.

THE ARRANGEMENT

It was a torpid night in summer, a storm threatening. I was sitting in a café in Paris explaining the arrangement to a young woman friend—Gisela is her name. She was eager for advice—her wedding was just days away—and I am a long married, sexually experienced woman. She had asked to meet me to have a talk, her mother long deceased, and so on.

The moon was buried under clouds, the sky was bleak, bleaker in fact than the word gunmetal would suggest. Bleaker than the expression starless night, though there were no stars visible that night. I was in the midst of a love affair but I was no longer in love. I was trying to explain.

The years will pass quickly, I began, and your innocence and passion will fade. There will be an arrangement.

I knew I was being cruel when I said this, that Gisela was still ecstatic, and would never forgive me. I will see you at the wedding, she said, and walked away. A fire engine howled in the distance.

I sat for a while and finished my cigarette. The air was stifling and stale with losses.

GENERIC LETTER TO
A LOVER FAR AWAY #4

Dear Lover Lover Lover Far Away,

I looked for you in Paris, I looked for you in Rome, I traveled to the Greek Island we loved together and now I ask you for advice about the moon and the gunmetal sky that descends in London and Paris as winter approaches and where I rest my bunions in little hotels by the water, what water does not matter—a river, an estuary, the sea. Some years have passed eventfully or uneventfully since my last communication and I have found this PO address among my chaotic belongings and I am not even certain if it is yours. Is it? If only we were still tribal, our obligations would be clear. We could not love, dear lover, and then discard.

Sincerely,

_____

APHRODITE
after a painting by Botticelli

One day, as she was emerging from the foamy bath and standing in front of him with her eyelids pulled back, the retinas exposed, he spoke of his decision. There was nothing between them but the puddle at her feet and the abandoned shell. She backed away, the sea at her back, the shell's scalloped edge cutting her heels. His face was stone, emptied of love.

She asked, "Why has Apollo chosen this moment to return me to the sea?"

But he did not reply.

She swam to the horizon and then beyond. Her wounded heart, a viscous fluid, once again became a jelly fish.

6. CARPE DIEM

WHAT WE LEARN FROM CRANES

Wait until low tide before stepping out onto the estuary. Walk slowly and with attention to the muddy ground. Remain light of foot. Turn away from the setting sun and then back again into its cooling rays. Rest in the grasses along the embankment. Take flight as the tide returns.

A COMFORTING STORY

Welcome to another comforting story. The setting: a sun which is a red ball flaring over the western sky beyond the mountains. There was a storm earlier in the day and storm clouds are still visible in the distance. We are driving to the mall which is in a valley surrounded by cliffs and there are birds riding the updrafts over the tree line, the mountains and forests dense with life. Hikers are sitting in their cars waiting for the storm's final retreat and deer are crouching under bushes. Two baby raccoons are splattered on the road and their spirits are playing in the wind. You remember the dead snake on the porch and the felled birch tree still fresh with sap on the other side of the retaining wall, how you sat on that wall with friends sucking on the whittled branches of that tree. Pulsing and fast you grew to adulthood on that wall.

MOUNTAINTOP

I would like to feel the top of a mountain, to inhale deeply the sweet thin air and fly in the updraft of a glacier's path. My lover is on top of the mountain. He sheds his clothes and falls backwards into the stars. I build a house on top of the mountain with no boundaries and no inflections, rooms opening to the heart of the earth. By midnight I am throbbing like a toad's throat. This is my mountain top of supple flesh and sparkling tears, soft as a newborn's touch.

A STORY ABOUT A LAMP

I was carrying a simple, blue, ceramic lamp down the street. The lamp had a big, round bottom and a white shade tipping one way and then another way in the wind. I held the bottom with one hand and the shade with the other and kept walking. I was pleased I'd thought to remove the bulb, but still annoyed by the wind and the lamp's awkwardness.

It was rush hour and the street was crowded. I heard a voice say, "Excuse me," but didn't know where it was coming from. Then again, "Excuse me," very persistent and desperate, I thought. Was it a beggar, one of the homeless vagabonds that sleep on the church stoop opposite by apartment building and haunt the neighborhood? Then I felt someone at my back. I spun around and almost hit her with the lamp.

It was a woman wearing a pink scarf. She had white hair and her face was cherubic, her expression sane.

"Where did you get that lamp, if you don't mind my asking?"

She spoke softly with a slight accent.

"Are you British?" I asked.

That would have made her even more sane and attractive to me. Luckily she said, "yes."

"Well, do you remember Conran's?" I asked.

"Oh yes," she said. "Is it from there?"

"Years ago when I lived in London," I said.

"Oh well," she said. "Everything has too much decoration these days. I want something plain."

"Yes, plain. Plain indeed," I said, thinking of the ways in which I was divesting to simplify my life.

Then there was a pause. The wind was blowing and it was cold. The woman with the pink scarf looked longingly at the lamp. It was though she had stepped out of my past to claim me and, for an instant, I wanted to give her the lamp in recognition of this, but I had promised the lamp to my daughter.

One way or another, it wasn't mine any more. I had passed it on.

WINNING SCRABBLE MOVES

XI

ZA

EL

EM

DO RE MI FA SO LA TI DO

SNOW

Wet ground covers the bear's den at the back of the garden. I say to myself: if only the snow would stop, if only the sun would rise. All this at three in the morning.

False spring, he had appeared briefly, his dark hair matted with twaddle and spit. He swatted at the squirrel foraging under the bird feeder, then found last summer's nest, the remnants of cardinal's eggs, the snowman's carrot nose, its lower body blanketed in drift.

Dogs howl like coyotes, coyotes like dogs. A family of chipmunks rattle the eaves, a snake is curled under the belly of the cold wood stove. Down by the farm an old man, a neighbor, a friend, emerges from a self-imposed hibernation reluctant to speak. In the distance, just over his right shoulder, the frozen groundhogs lie prostrate inside their tunnels. He steps on them in his dreams and hears them pop. Keep walking to the pond, he says, collect the pods as mulch, remove your shoes as you enter the mudroom and wipe what you have seen from your mind. There is no way to stop the snow or shift the season, no way to return to sleep. Even a poet's words are impotent against the searing wind and the ice particles forming on the wilted geraniums.

Now comes the junco with his black upper body chirping his winter song and the red-bellied woodpecker sounding like a whale. Why do some seasons feel too short and others too long? They arrive and we complain, vanquished by nature and nature's intention.

REMEMBERING A RECIPE WITH DANNON YOGURT

Red lettering on a white ground in a waxed container about the size of a coffee cup. No need to decant the luscious contents. Eat a few bites and then add a chopped peeled carrot. Crunch and slurp.

SYMPHONY

We were walking across the reservoir at mid-day into the bald eagle preserve and we were quiet and kept moving, as the sign instructed. Bold black letters on a yellow ground, covered in plastic, the sign didn't belong in the preserve, we thought. These precious birds, everyone knew they were nesting up in the highest tree, mountains on all sides, a steep embankment, driftwood along the edges. The preserve was a cathedral of hope and we were reverent without a sign telling us to be reverent. We knew what awaited us if we remained patient. We walked slowly and then we rested on a quarried rock, white with brown flecks. There were four of us; no one spoke.

The tallest pine on the peninsula held the nest, visible to the naked eye. We spotted a bird, but said nothing. We didn't shout, or point, or remonstrate. The bird was flying and we could see it clearly: a white head, long legs grasping a chipmunk or a mouse. It wasn't as big as we'd imagined, but it was grand, gliding past us, indifferent to us, like a teenager strutting its stuff.

It will always remain a mystery why the eagle flew so close to us that day. It was like listening to a symphony that echoes within us for the rest of our lives.

LIFECYCLE RIME

Water to water dust to dust stopping on water as we must.

Whose waves they are we think we know the riptides flow beneath us slow.

We stand aloft we stop and go as riptides flow beneath us slow.

All together now: Water to water dust to dust stopping on water as we must.

ON THE GREEN

You're walking along the golf course towards the sound—
you and your golfing friends—early spring, late afternoon,
fading light, and there's an old man on a bed in the middle of
the green waiting for you. His hair is white and so is his skin
and he continually rises from the bed to putt and swing.
Some say it's a miracle he is still alive and still golfing. He
needs a caddy but there are none available, they have all
disappeared, so he waits for you as his last recourse, the only
person on the green who might be willing to carry his clubs.
He smiles as you approach and you think: He looks familiar
but what is he doing here? The old man is singing, bursting
with story and song. You can hear the words clearly: *Play
on.*

TRUST THE WIND

In the beginning, everything is want: a devouring sea, a suckling breast, desire. Later, the skin enclosing our body tires. We are vexed.

Trust the wind. Slide with the curling wave as it pours onto a sandy beach, pebble and shells rattling like a turtle smiling at dawn.

Trust the wind. Do not retreat into redoubts and caves. Rise into the flickering light. Observe the dragonfly's wings. Observe a buttercup.

-end-

Made in the USA
Charleston, SC
07 December 2014